T0023657

WHAT IF YOU WERE ON THE RUSSIAN FRONT IN WORLD WAR II?

AN INTERACTIVE HISTORY ADVENTURE

by Matt Doeden

CAPSTONE PRESS
a capstone imprint

Published by You Choose, an imprint of Capstone
1710 Roe Crest Drive, North Mankato, Minnesota 56003
capstonepub.com

Library of Congress Cataloging-in-Publication Data is available on the Library of
Congress website.

ISBN 9781666390919 (hardcover)
ISBN 9781666390902 (paperback)
ISBN 9781666391060 (ebook PDF)

Summary: Takes readers through a series of choices placing them in the midst of
the action of World War II on the Russian front.

Editorial Credits
Editor: Mandy Robbins; Designer: Hilary Wacholz; Media Researcher: Jo Miller;
Production Specialist: Tori Abraham

Image Credits
Alamy: 502 collection, 99, carlo maggio, 78, Geopix, 95, Pictorial Press Ltd, 40,
Smith Archive, 50; Avalon/Berliner Verlag, 39; Getty Images: bruev, 11, 26,
picture alliance, 4, Roger Viollet, 61, Sovfoto, 34, 44, 49, 56, 66, 75, ullstein bild
Dtl., 12, Universal History Archive, 87, Zeferli, Cover; Shutterstock: David
Peinado Romero, 105, Everett Collection, Cover, 1, 101, high fliers, 93, Radowitz,
28, Red_Baron, 106, RolandsBoss, 24, samray, 71, Szymon Bartosz, 21, Valentyn
Volkov, 9; Wikimedia: Public Domain, 53

Design Elements
Shutterstock: Roman Amanov

TABLE OF CONTENTS

German soldiers advancing on the Russian front during World War II

ABOUT YOUR ADVENTURE

YOU are on the front lines of World War II (1939–1945). The war started in Europe with Nazi Germany's attack on Poland, then spread throughout the continent. By 1941, Japan had attacked the United States naval base in Hawaii on the side of the Axis powers. Japan is seeking domination in the Pacific. Now Germany is on the move. The Nazis are launching a full-scale invasion of the western part of the Soviet Union.

You are charged with defending your homeland from the invaders. How will you fight? What choices will you make? YOU CHOOSE the path to follow. Will you succeed at your mission or fail and let your country down?

• Turn the page to begin your adventure.

CHAPTER 1
A LOOMING THREAT

The hum of airplane engines roars above eastern Europe. Massive tanks rumble across the landscape. Battles rage at sea, on land, and in the air as Germany and the Axis powers march toward the Soviet Union. The Allied forces, including Great Britain, France, and the Soviet Union, are doing their best to push them back.

You shake your head. People are dying by the hundreds of thousands. And not just soldiers. Civilians are suffering and dying as well.

"What is it all for?" you ask yourself. The world has changed so much in the past few years.

Your life in the Soviet Union was never easy. The government, under leader Joseph Stalin, has not always helped its citizens. But this . . . this is different. The enemy is bent on total domination. They won't settle for anything less than a full surrender.

So, you've done the only thing you can. You've taken up arms to defend yourself and the people you love. The enemy is strong. You may not survive the fight. But you are ready. You button your uniform. You check your weapon. You take a breath and step forward, ready to do what it takes to push back the German invaders.

- To serve as a Soviet scout, turn to page 8.
- To captain a torpedo boat on the Black Sea, turn to page 37.
- To attack German supply lines, turn to page 65.

CHAPTER 2

RELAYING THE MESSAGE

"I could get used to being out here," says Viktor, as he looks up at a bright blue sky.

You smile and nod. You're in the foothills of the Carpathian Mountains near the border of Ukraine and Poland. All you hear is a gentle breeze, birds chirping, and the crunch of your own footsteps as you move across the land. "Yes, you can almost forget that we're surrounded by death and war."

Turn the page.

But as nice as it is out here, this is no pleasure hike. You and Viktor are members of the Soviet Union's Red Army, and you're on a scouting mission. It's the summer of 1942, and Nazi forces are gathering for an invasion. According to your commanders, the Nazis are expected to march on Moscow, the capital of the Soviet Union. Your job is to gather as much information as you can about the size and location of the enemy force.

You're well suited to life as a scout. You grew up in the mountains, hunting and tracking animals for food. You know how to move unseen, how to track, and your military training gives you expertise in what enemy forces are up to. The Red Army is relying on good intelligence to prepare for the coming battle. It's critical that you find out all you can. Viktor is new to scouting. He's learning the ropes at your side.

For several days, you and Viktor move through the mountains. Finally, you spot what you're looking for. Smoke on the horizon. You move in, remaining hidden in the trees as you seek high ground.

Turn the page.

"There they are," Viktor whispers. You're perched atop a rock ledge on the north face of a mountain. Your height gives you an excellent view of the flatter land that stretches out before you. It's filled with soldiers, tanks, and other vehicles.

Nazi troops and tanks

"Look at where they're going," you reply. "They're marching southeast."

"Yes," Viktor says. He doesn't understand why that's important.

"Think, Viktor. Moscow is northeast. They're not marching in the right direction."

Viktor laughs. "Ha! They're lost!"

You shake your head. "No. I'm afraid they know exactly where they're headed. They're not going to Moscow. This path leads them directly to Stalingrad."

Viktor shakes his head. "But nobody is expecting that. They won't be ready for a force of this size."

Turn the page.

Now he understands. Everything the Red Army thinks they know about the coming attack is wrong. They shouldn't be preparing Moscow for battle. They should be preparing Stalingrad.

It's critical information. You have to get it back to your commanders as soon as possible. Just then, a shot rings out.

"We've been spotted!" Viktor shouts. Another shot pings off nearby rocks. Both of you scramble to get away from the ledge and into the safety of the trees. But Viktor trips over a rock. He yells as he tumbles down a steep slope.

Viktor has slid down at least 40 feet onto a completely exposed shelf on the mountainside. You can tell that his leg is broken. He doesn't stand a chance down there.

Should you help him? It would be incredibly dangerous to attempt a rescue, and the information you have is too important to risk both of your lives. But can you just leave him there for the Germans to pick off? The thought makes you shudder.

- To help Viktor, turn to page 16.
- To escape with the information, turn to page 18.

Your first instinct is to help your fellow soldier. Without giving it much thought, you step out and scramble down the steep, rocky incline.

Shots ring out as you reach Viktor. He's conscious, but in a lot of pain. One look at his leg tells you why. It's a bad break. His left leg is completely useless.

Viktor cries out in pain as you try to drag him back up the slope. If you can just get over the ledge and out of range of German fire, maybe you can save him. You heave him with every bit of strength you have.

But Viktor is heavier than you, and the slope is steep. A shot zips past you, blasting into the rock face of the mountain. It was just inches from your head. You groan as you try to pull Viktor up.

"Go!" he groans. Sweat drips off his face. "Even if you get me up there, I can't run. We'll both be captured. You have to get the information back to our commanders."

You know that leaving Viktor here means he'll be a prisoner of war at the very least. You don't want to abandon your friend, but he's right. Your commanders need that information.

- To give up on the rescue, turn to page 18.
- To keep trying to save him, turn to page 25.

There's nothing you can do. Viktor's leg is shattered. Even if you could pull him to cover, he'd never escape. You have to get this information to your commanders.

"I'm sorry," you tell him. Viktor nods, trying to mask the pain on his face. He understands. He knows what's at stake.

With a final glance over your shoulder, you dash back under the cover of the trees. The Germans will follow, so you run as fast as you can, south into rough mountain terrain.

You've spent lots of time in the mountains. You know how to move quickly and safely. For the next hour, you put as much distance as you can between yourself and the enemy. You make camp for the night, pitching a small tarp against a thick stand of trees and building a very small fire, and consider your options.

You could head straight east. That would take you to Soviet-held territory the fastest. But you'd be traveling on open ground, with a greater chance of being spotted by enemy troops. Or you could go south before cutting east. It's a slower route but should take you farther from the German lines.

Time is critical. Every hour matters. Is it worth the risk to deliver the message faster?

- To go east, turn to page 20.
- To head south first, turn to page 22.

You stake out across the open plains, headed due east. It's a more dangerous course. But every moment matters.

As you move east, you see signs of the enemy. Smoke hangs in the sky not far to your north. At one point, you spot a German patrol scouting the terrain. You stay low and out of sight, and soon enough it passes.

You've got some rations in your pack, but you're running low. Moving as fast as you're able takes a lot of energy, and your stomach rumbles. So when you spot a deer in a nearby meadow, you consider your options.

You're a skilled hunter. You're confident you could shoot the deer and make a meal of it. But it would be risky. The sound of a gunshot or the smoke from a fire could attract attention.

Still, you are tired and hungry. Your body needs energy. Is it worth the risk to make yourself stronger?

- To ignore the deer, turn to page 23.
- To hunt the deer, turn to page 26.

You can't risk another encounter with enemy forces. If you're captured or killed, the Red Army will have that much less time to prepare Stalingrad for attack. So you forge a path south, through the rough terrain of the Carpathian foothills. The Germans are coming in huge numbers. They'll take the easiest path. There's little chance you'll encounter enemy forces here.

Your progress is slow as you travel over the rocky terrain. The next day, you move out of the foothills and head east across the plains. You come across a small farm. It looks like there are people there. Are they friendly to the Allied cause? Or are they still here because they have German loyalties? There's no way to be sure. You'll have to make a choice.

- To approach the farm, turn to page 32.
- To steer clear, turn to page 35.

You take a long look at the deer grazing in the distance. Food would be great. You can almost smell the venison cooking over an open fire. Just the thought makes your stomach growl and your mouth water. But attracting attention behind enemy lines could turn into a death sentence. You just can't take the risk. So you press on, trekking ever eastward toward friendly territory.

The sky darkens as you cross the open plains of Ukraine. A gentle rain begins to fall. Soon, that rain turns into a downpour. You slog over muddy ground, soaking wet, as torrents of rain pelt you.

A small house stands in the distance. It looks abandoned. There are no lights, and part of the roof is sagging. An antenna sticks out of the damaged roof. It looks like it is about to tip over.

Turn the page.

It's not much, but it could get you out of the rain. Is it time to rest and get dry? Or should you press on, regardless of the conditions?

- To stop at the house, turn to page 28.
- To keep going through the storm, turn to page 31.

"I can't leave you here," you answer. You grab Viktor and heave him up the slope. He cries out in agony as his leg twists against the ground. Your progress is not quick enough. An enemy shot catches you in the arm. You double over in pain, and both of you slide back down the slope.

You realize too late that rescue was hopeless. You try to scramble back up, but with a bad arm, you're too slow. Six German soldiers rush up the slope to you, their rifles drawn. "Drop your weapon," one man says with a smirk.

You have no choice but to surrender. You are now a prisoner of war. Life in a German prison camp will not be easy. But at least you are alive.

THE END

To follow another path, turn to page 7.
To learn more about the Russian front, turn to page 97.

It could take days to get back to Soviet-held territory. You need energy. It's worth the risk.

The sound of your rifle echoes across the countryside. You wince, hoping that you're far enough away from enemy forces that they won't hear the shot. There's no time to waste. You get to work, preparing several large cuts of meat over a small fire. The smell makes your mouth water.

But sound carries a long way on the open plains. And the loud pop of your rifle reached a group of nearby German soldiers. When they come to investigate, they catch you off guard.

In your surprise, you grab for your weapon. That's a mistake. The German soldiers might have just taken you prisoner. But the moment you grab for your rifle, they respond.

Someone is going to enjoy the feast you're preparing. But it won't be you.

THE END

To follow another path, turn to page 7.
To learn more about the Russian front, turn to page 97.

You're not making much ground in these conditions. You need to get out of the rain. So you head for the house.

You were right. It's abandoned. It looks like someone left in a hurry. Random items are scattered on the floor. You manage to find a small lantern and a few cans of food. As you open one, something else catches your eye. There in the corner stands a large radio with a transmitter.

World War II German field radio

You don't waste any time. The transmitter is battery operated, and you're in luck. It has a charge. You quickly tune to a frequency used by the Red Army, hoping it will be strong enough.

"Hello," you say into the microphone. You give your name and rank. "Can anyone hear me?"

There's a moment of silence. Then the radio crackles. "We receive you," replies a voice. It's a radio operator with the Red Army!

You relay all of the information you've collected as quickly as you can, knowing that the batteries in your transmitter could die at any moment.

"Message received," confirms the radio operator. "I'll bring this to my commander immediately. Good luck soldier. Get yourself back to friendly territory."

Turn the page.

You let out a sigh of relief. You've done your job. You still have to get back to safety. But no matter what, you've given the Red Army a chance in what will surely be one of the bloodiest battles in the war.

Satisfied that you've done your duty, you curl up on a small bed in the corner of the room and drift off into a well-deserved sleep. Tomorrow, you'll be up at the crack of dawn to make your way back to friendly territory.

THE END

To follow another path, turn to page 7.
To learn more about the Russian front, turn to page 97.

You shake your head. "Just keep moving," you mutter to yourself.

The wind howls and the rain pours down in sheets as you slog over muddy ground. Visibility is so poor that you don't even notice a group of tents in front of you until it's too late.

"Identify yourself!" shouts a voice in German. You realize your mistake too late. You've just stumbled into a Nazi camp.

You turn and run. It's your best chance. It might be your only chance. But it's not good enough. A shot rings out. You feel a flash of pain in your back. You fall face-first onto the muddy plains of Ukraine. This is where your story ends.

THE END

To follow another path, turn to page 7.
To learn more about the Russian front, turn to page 97.

You're moving too slowly. Your route south has cost you valuable time. Maybe someone here can help. They might have a vehicle you could use, or food. So you approach the farm carefully. A middle-aged woman stands outside, tending a small garden. She yelps, startled to see you.

You put your hands in the air and call out to her in Russian. Suddenly, she relaxes and walks toward you.

"You're Red Army," she observes. "At first, I feared you were German. I don't know what I would have done."

The woman, Alla, gives you a warm welcome and insists you come inside for food. As much as you don't want to slow down, your rumbling stomach aches for food. While you eat, you tell her that you need to get back to friendly territory fast to deliver a critical message.

Alla grins. "I think I can help you." She leads you out to a small barn. Inside, a gray mare is munching on hay. "Take the horse," Alla says. "It's my part in the war effort."

With a quick thank-you, and a promise to return the horse if you are able to, you're off. On horseback, you cover ground at a much quicker pace. Within a day, you see a welcome site—the Soviet flag flying over a Red Army camp. As you ride in, you know you've accomplished your mission.

Viktor gave his life to make this possible. You just hope his sacrifice is worth it.

THE END

To follow another path, turn to page 7.
To learn more about the Russian front, turn to page 97.

You take a long look at the farm. This feels a great distance from the battle lines. But you just don't know who you can trust. All you can do is press forward.

By foot, it's a slow journey. You steer clear of any type of settlement, never knowing where the German forces might be in control. It takes almost five days before you cross into Soviet-held territory and connect with a Red Army brigade.

Your report is no surprise. "Yes, we learned of this two days ago," explains the brigade's commander. "Preparations for battle have begun. We're glad to have you back. We'll need every able fighter we can get to stop the German advance."

Turn the page.

You leave dejected. If you'd been faster, the Red Army could have had days more to prepare for what will surely be a pivotal battle in the war. Instead, Viktor's sacrifice and all your work were for nothing. The Germans are coming, and you know a terrible, bloody battle awaits. You only hope you can survive it.

THE END

To follow another path, turn to page 7.

To learn more about the Russian front, turn to page 97.

CHAPTER 3
BATTLE ON THE BLACK SEA

The year is 1941. It's a quiet day. The waters of the Black Sea are calm, and you stand on the deck of a Soviet torpedo boat. The small boat—about 60 feet long—carries a crew of you and six other men. You're part of the Soviet Union's Black Sea Fleet, charged with controlling the strategic waters and patrolling its shores.

"Keep a sharp watch," you order Lev, one of your officers. "The Axis powers are pushing farther and farther into Soviet territory. We can't let our guard down for a moment."

Turn the page.

"Yes, Captain," Lev replies. He leaves you standing alone near the front, or bow, of the ship. You have a bad feeling. This is your first naval command, and it comes at a time when World War II is raging across eastern Europe.

You're on your way back from a supply mission to the city of Odessa, along the northwestern shore of the Black Sea. There, Allied forces are surrounded by the enemy.

You're doing everything you can to help hold off the Axis advances. Controlling the Black Sea is a big part of that. You know that you can't let the enemy take over this critical waterway.

Suddenly, you hear a low humming sound. It takes you a moment to realize that it's coming from above. "Air attack!" you shout.

You and your crew scramble. Lev and
Aleksey man the boat's two machine guns
while you take the controls, knowing that
a moving target will be harder for Axis bombers
to hit. The boat's motor hums as you bring it
up to speed.

A Nazi speedboat on the Black Sea

Turn the page.

The enemy aircraft appear overhead. Dive bombers are dropping explosives. The chatter of machine guns fills the air. Soon, the sky is filled with German planes. The Axis navy is no match for the Soviet navy. But what they lack in sea power they more than make up for in air superiority.

German Junker Ju 87 Stuka dive bombers

You scan the water around you. The main fleet sits off of your port, or left, side. It includes the bigger warships, such as destroyers and cruisers.

"Should we move in tighter?" asks Pavel, who is second-in-command.

Perhaps being closer to the main fleet would give you some protection. On the other hand, the enemy is probably targeting the biggest ships. Moving in closer might only put you in the line of fire.

Either choice comes with risks. But this is war. Safety isn't always an option.

- To move in closer to the fleet, turn to page 42.
- To head away from the fleet, turn to page 44.

"Hard to port," you call out, warning your crew of your sudden change of direction. The enemy air strike is in full force. Explosions rock several of the ships in the fleet. Bombs explode on the water, kicking up huge waves. A moment ago, it was a clear, calm day. Now you find yourself navigating through a haze of smoke on a choppy sea.

You bring your smaller torpedo boat in close to the bigger ships. "Tuck in next to that cruiser," Lev calls out. An Admiral Nakhimov-class cruiser cuts through the water, its guns firing. At more than 500 feet long, the cruiser dwarfs your little torpedo boat. Maybe nobody will target you when you're so close to such a powerful ship.

You hang off the stern of the big cruiser as the air strike continues. All around you, ships of the Soviet's Black Sea Fleet are burning.

You also watch as some of the enemy aircraft are shot down. They crash into the water, sending huge waves out in every direction,

Then everything changes. A bomb strikes the cruiser. Metal fragments from the explosion rip through the hull of your boat.

"We're taking on water!" shouts Pavel. He's right. The damage to your boat is huge.

"Abandon ship!" you call out. There's nothing you can do. Your boat is going to sink. Acting quickly, you and your crew grab and deploy an inflatable life raft. Within a minute, you're sitting in the raft, watching your boat slip beneath the choppy surface of the Black Sea.

"Where do we go, Captain?" Lev asks.

- To head for the cruiser, turn to page 46.
- To paddle toward open water, turn to page 48.

"Hard to starboard," you call out, telling your crew that you're turning the boat right, away from the rest of the fleet. "The enemy will be targeting the bigger ships. We need to put some distance between us and them."

Your boat speeds away as the battle rages all around. Machine guns chatter from the decks of Soviet warships. Bombs from the Axis planes rock their targets. Smoke rises from the deck of a nearby destroyer. A gaping hole in the hull of the ship shows that a bomb has hit its target.

"That destroyer is going to sink," Aleksey says. He's right. Already you can see a frantic effort from the crew to abandon ship. Where the hull is burning, men are throwing themselves off of the deck and into the water.

"We should go back," Aleksey says. "We can help." Going back would put you and your crew at huge risk. The fire could spread if there's a fuel leak. The sinking ship could suck you down with it. Do you dare try?

- To go back and help, turn to page 50.
- To remain where you are until the ship sinks, turn to page 52.

In the middle of a battle, this little raft feels so small. It's terrifying, and all you want is to be on board a bigger ship. "Let's get to that cruiser," you say.

You use the life raft's little paddles to slowly move toward the bigger ship. But before you can get there, a deafening sound rocks the water all around you. Your little raft is tossed by the explosion of an enemy bomb. In an instant, you're in the cold water, desperately trying to keep your head above the churning waves.

Lev and a few of the others are clinging to the side of the raft. But the blast tossed Aleksey farther away. He appears to be unconscious. You start to swim toward him, but making progress in the choppy water is difficult. The sounds of war around you fade as the attack ends. But you're still battling to get to your fellow officer.

Aleksey doesn't respond when you call
out his name. You grab him by the arm. He's
bleeding from a bad cut on his head. He needs
help now, but there's nothing you can do.
In the cold, choppy waters of the Black Sea,
you're fighting just to keep yourself afloat.
Do you have the strength to pull Aleksey
along with you?

- To support Aleksey here and wait for help, turn to page 57.

- To try to pull him back to the raft, turn to page 59.

The attack is chaos. All around you, bombs are exploding. Machine gun fire cuts through the sky. And all you have is a small life raft. You have to protect yourself and your men. You must get as far away from the fighting as possible. You'll wait out the battle and hope somebody finds you and your men after it's over.

Your plan to get clear of the battle is flawed, however. The lifeboat and its little paddles can barely move in the choppy Black Sea. You're tossed and turned as the battle rages around you. As the bombs drop, another small torpedo boat spots you and quickly motors to your position. You climb aboard, where a young captain helps you onto the deck.

"We're in bad shape," he says. "Four of my crew are wounded. I need someone to man the machine gun. Can you do it?"

You're exhausted. Can you even operate a machine gun right now? Your arms are weak from paddling. Maybe you should ask one of your men to man the gun so you can rest for a moment. The captain looks at you. You want to do everything you can. Do you man the gun, or should you let someone else do it?

- To man the gun, turn to page 60.
- To decline, turn to page 63.

You don't hesitate. Even as enemy planes drop
their bombs all around you, you turn and head
right back into the heart of the danger.

"Both sides, watch for survivors!" you call out.
As you get closer to the damaged destroyer, you
see the sheen of oil on the water. A single spark
could set the whole thing ablaze.

"There," calls Pavel. He's spotted a single survivor struggling in the water. He doesn't have a life preserver, and he's working hard to stay afloat.

"I've got three men over here," Aleksey replies. A quick glance shows you three men, all wearing life preservers.

You've got to make a quick decision. Who do you save first? A single man in more danger, or three men who might have a better chance on their own?

- To save the single man, turn to page 54.
- To head for the three men, turn to page 55.

"Hold position," you order. "It's too risky. We'll go back when the fighting is over."

The air strike continues for several more long and terrifying minutes. But then it's over as quickly as it began. Set apart from the fleet, you survey the damage from afar.

It's a devastating blow. The Axis attack has sunk several ships and damaged many more. Finally, after waiting a few minutes, you decide that it's finally safe enough to head back to help rescue the sailors who had to abandon their ships.

You're too late to help some of the unlucky men. But you do manage to pull five survivors out of the water. The attack has left the Black Sea Fleet badly weakened.

As you begin your voyage back to port with survivors on board, you find yourself wishing that you'd done more. You feel like you were little more than a spectator to this crushing attack in the German advance into the Soviet Union.

THE END

To follow another path, turn to page 7.
To learn more about the Russian front, turn to page 97.

a Soviet light cruiser

"He's not going to make it much longer," you say, pointing to the man without the life preserver. You steer the boat toward him, slowing down just as you reach him.

You're not a moment too soon. The man is exhausted. You pull him into the boat, where he gasps for breath. But there's no time to stop. The air attack is over. But the aftermath is devastating. You keep going, saving the other three men and almost a dozen more sailors before the waters are once again quiet.

It was a bitter defeat for the Black Sea Fleet today. Your control over the critical waterway was badly weakened. But you did all you could, and your efforts have saved lives.

THE END

To follow another path, turn to page 7.
To learn more about the Russian front, turn to page 97.

"That way," you order. You want to save as many lives as you can. You have to go to where there are three men, instead of just one.

As you reach them, the final enemy aircraft disappear over the horizon. The attack is over.

Because each man is wearing a life preserver, the rescue is simple. They're cold and tired, but in otherwise good condition.

Once they're on board, you turn toward the single man. You can just make out his head above the waves.

You turn and steer toward him, going as fast as you can. But just before you reach him, you see his head slip beneath the surface. He doesn't come back up. Your heart sinks as you realize that you've lost him.

Turn the page.

You continue working to save as many lives as you can. But you know that the image of that one sailor being swallowed by the Black Sea will never leave you. He's a man you never met and whose name you'll never know. But his memory will haunt you for the rest of your life.

THE END

To follow another path, turn to page 7.
To learn more about the Russian front, turn to page 97.

You can barely keep yourself above water. The idea of trying to pull an unconscious man back to the drifting raft is impossible. So you do the only thing you can. You grab Aleksey under the arms and float together on your backs.

The waves wash over you as you look to the sky. The enemy planes are gone now. Smoke billows from fires to the damaged warships. You can hear engines humming and distant voices.

You hold that position on your back, supporting Aleksey. It's a position that spends very little energy, allowing you to use your body's reserves to keep itself warm and afloat.

After what seems like hours, rescue comes. It's actually the crew of another torpedo boat that arrives to save you.

Turn the page.

"You're going to make it," says a young sailor, as he helps you onto the deck. You're alive. Aleksey is alive, although he's in bad shape. And the rest of your crew made it as well.

That's more than a lot of your fellow sailors can say. It was a bloody day on the Black Sea. The Soviet Black Sea Fleet took heavy losses, and it may never fully recover. But despite all of that, you're one of the lucky ones to have survived it.

THE END

To follow another path, turn to page 7.
To learn more about the Russian front, turn to page 97.

You know help will come. But you're not sure if he'll make it without medical attention soon. You try to drag Aleksey back to the raft. You quickly grow tired. Aleksey is still unconscious, so you're trying to drag his full weight along with your own.

The currents carry the raft away from you faster than you can swim for it. You keep going, but it's hopeless. As you realize your situation, panic sets in. Your energy is spent. Your body temperature is dropping.

Rescue will come. But it will not come quickly enough for you or Aleksey. The Black Sea Fleet has lost a lot of good sailors today. Sadly, you're one of them.

THE END

To follow another path, turn to page 7.
To learn more about the Russian front, turn to page 97.

You're tired. You're hurting. And the shame of losing your boat hangs over you. But this is war, and you can't quit. You pull yourself to your feet. "Let's get some Nazis," you say with a groan.

The captain smiles and clasps your shoulder. "You're my kind of sailor," he says.

It's been awhile since you operated a machine gun. But once you step behind the powerful weapon, it all comes back to you. The *pop-pop-popping* of bullets is like a rhythm, and you quickly find your groove.

When one enemy plane swoops low to drop a bomb on a nearby battleship, you're ready. You open fire. Your shot is on target, clipping the wing of the bomber. It spins out of control and crashes into the dark waters of the Black Sea.

The air attack doesn't last long. Soon, the Axis planes have finished dropping their bombs. They rise into the sky and disappear over the horizon. They leave a path of destruction behind. Dozens of ships are damaged. Several have been destroyed completely. You join in the rescue effort, pulling more sailors from the sea.

Turn the page.

It was a costly day on the Black Sea. But you did everything you could. You hope the fighting spirit of the Soviet navy will carry on. It's going to be a long and bloody war. But now you know you have what it takes to protect your homeland and defeat the invading army.

THE END

To follow another path, turn to page 7.
To learn more about the Russian front, turn to page 97.

You shake your head. "No. I'm too tired," you explain.

Aleksey steps up. He's been paddling too. He's just as exhausted as you are. But he doesn't let that stop him. "I'll do it," he says.

You collapse on the deck, feeling defeated. Your boat is lost. What's the point of continuing to fight?

You watch as the rest of your crew pitches in. They each do what they can to fight off the attackers. Aleksey even manages to shoot down one of the enemy planes.

Then, just as suddenly as it started, the attack is over. The Black Sea Fleet is badly damaged. You've lost a lot of big warships. But almost everyone kept fighting—everyone but you.

Turn the page.

The heroic efforts of others managed to stave off the attack. Many ships are destroyed or damaged . . . but others survived, thanks to the men who fought to defend them.

You know your days as a captain are over. When things got tough, you gave up. No one will ever forget that, especially you. Maybe the Black Sea Fleet will be stronger without you.

THE END

To follow another path, turn to page 7.
To learn more about the Russian front, turn to page 97.

CHAPTER 4

ATTACKING THE SUPPLY LINES

"Stay down," whispers Yelena, motioning with her hands to stay tucked behind the overturned truck that lies in front of you. The ground rumbles as a train approaches.

"Look at it," Yelena says with a gasp. Car after car passes. "It's loaded with food, weapons, ammunition, fuel . . . everything the Nazis need."

You nod. You've been scouting Nazi supply lines for weeks. As the German army marches east into Russia, it needs huge shipments of supplies. Some come by truck.

Turn the page.

Lately, much of it comes by train. And many of those shipments come through your country of Belarus. The Nazis control all the railways from this point west, and they're using them to fuel the invasion.

You watch for a few minutes more as the train rolls by. Then you and Yelena head back, meeting up with your small troop of fighters, called partisans, in a secret wooded area.

Partisan fighters planning an attack

As partisans, you're not part of any formal military. You're just civilians who have come together to fight against the German advance into your homelands. You have little interaction with the Russian Red Army, which is doing most of the direct combat. Partisans focus more on missions that disrupt enemy operations. While you do receive some objectives, intelligence, and supplies from the military, you're not part of the military yourselves.

Back at your little base, you meet up with several other fellow soldiers. One of them, Pyotr, is the leader of your group. But Pyotr is the leader in name only. You operate as equals here. You make decisions together. You all know that every time you carry out an attack, you're risking your lives. With this group, it's less about giving orders and more about coming to group decisions.

Turn the page.

"We spotted an enemy convoy," Pyotr reports. "Dozens of trucks. They have to cross the Byarezina River to get east. If we could blow up the bridge there, it would completely block that supply route."

You glance at a big map of the area that Pyotr has spread out over a small table. He's right. Destroying the bridge would hinder the Germans. But there are other bridges. It would slow down shipments, but not stop them entirely.

Yelena stands and points to another spot on the map. "The Nazis are running trains east toward their frontline troops. We just saw one roll through. We're talking about really huge payloads. I say we hit the next train. We derail it completely. It will be an enormous loss for the enemy."

"That's a lot riskier," Pyotr points out. "Blowing up a bridge we can do on our own time and schedule. Trying to hit a moving train could expose us."

"We're here to hit the German supply lines," Yelena argues. "So let's get to it"

The group is split. They turn to you, waiting for the deciding vote.

- To blow up the bridge, turn to page 70.
- To try to derail the train, turn to page 72.

"I don't know if we're ready for a big attack on a train," you say. "Let's hit that bridge. Anything we can do to slow down the supply lines will make life tougher for the German army."

Yelena looks disappointed. She's a risk-taker. You prefer to play it safe.

You wait until after sunset to attack. Moving through the dark forest makes you almost impossible to spot. As you approach the bridge, you hear voices.

"Germans," whispers Pyotr. "They're scouting the route ahead."

You sit quietly, listening. "I think there's only two men," you say.

"We should capture them," Yelena suggests. "We can take them prisoner and then blow up the bridge."

Pyotr shakes his head. "What do we want with prisoners? No, let's just avoid them and stick to the plan."

- To try to take prisoners, turn to page 80.
- To wait until the patrol leaves, turn to page 82.

"Yelena is right," you decide. "Sure, trying to derail a Nazi train is a bigger risk. But this is war. If we want to make a difference, we need to take risks. What's the point of fighting at all if we don't do all we can to hurt the enemy?"

As you look around, the others nod their heads. The group, which includes a dozen fighters, has come to a decision. Now it's time for planning.

Pyotr quickly gets to work, outlining a plan of attack. Every train is accompanied by military protection. So one team will create a distraction to focus attention from the real attack. A second team will do the risky job of planting and detonating explosives just as the next train arrives. It's by far the riskiest part of the plan. The tracks are on flat, open ground with no cover.

If the distraction fails, it will be a death trap. Both groups will be small—just a few fighters. Bigger groups are more likely to attract attention.

Pyotr volunteers to lead the distraction team, while Yelena will lead the explosives team. The attack will come at dawn tomorrow. Which team will you join?

- To create a distraction, turn to page 74.
- To detonate the explosives, turn to page 77.

"The mission depends on us," Pyotr says the next morning. "Our goal is to set off an explosion that will get the attention of any guards with the train. While they investigate the explosion, Yelena's team will hit the target."

The sun is just rising in the eastern sky. A train carrying German supplies is set to roll through the area sometime this morning.

"The Germans have lost several of these trains to partisan attacks, so they're heavily guarded now," Pyotr reminds you. He pulls a grenade from his pack.

As partisan fighters, you do get some help from the Soviet Union's Red Army. These small explosives are part of one of the rare supply drops they provide. You know that your group has a very limited supply of explosives. You're putting a lot of what you have into this attack.

The two of you take position atop a heavily wooded ridge that overlooks the train tracks. About an hour later, you hear the distant *clack-clack-clacking* of an approaching train. Two military trucks guard the train on either side. Both are armed with large machine guns.

Turn the page.

"Yelena and her team are about a mile ahead," Pyotr says. You already know that, but Pyotr likes to talk when he's nervous. "Any guards that are with the train will be on high alert. Let's get their attention."

Pyotr throws the grenade behind the military trucks, into a nearby stand of trees. The idea is that the explosion will distract them from what's ahead. But a second passes. Two . . . three.

Pyotr curses. "It didn't go off! It was a dud!"

The train is going by. The distraction has failed. You have to do something! Do you want to try to distract the guards on the train or the truck drivers?

- To run toward the train firing your weapon, turn to page 84.
- To shout at the trucks, turn to page 85.

You smile at Yelena. "You don't think I'd let you do this without me, do you?"

The next morning you get up before dawn. As the sun rises, you prepare. Pyotr and Olga will use a grenade to create a distraction to whatever military protection comes with the train. You, Yelena, and Ivan will set an explosive charge and detonate it from a safe distance just as the train comes around a bend.

"That should be enough," Yelena says. "Our goal isn't to detonate the train itself. Instead, we'll destroy the tracks just before it arrives. Once one car comes off the rails, everything else will follow. As long as we're hidden away in the woods, they'll never spot us. It will be complete confusion for a few minutes. We can slip away before they have a chance to search for us."

Turn the page.

You move silently through a wooded area, taking up position near the tracks. Within an hour, you hear and feel the big train coming.

"Now we wait for Pyotr," you whisper. When you hear his grenade explode, it will be time to move. But you never hear it. You can see the smoke from the locomotive coming around the bend. Something went wrong!

"It's now or never!" Pyotr shouts. "Let's go!"

Pyotr and Ivan charge toward the tracks to set the charge. They're not willing to wait. For them, the chance to derail the train is worth it. Should you go help set the charge? Or might you be more useful here, providing cover fire for your fellow partisans?

- To join Pyotr and Ivan, turn to page 87.
- To stay here to provide cover fire, turn to page 89.

This time, you agree with Yelena. "They have no idea we're here," you say. "We can take them and still blow up the bridge. It's just one more way we can hurt the German army. We'd be fools not to take this chance."

Pyotr sighs but agrees to the plan. The two soldiers on patrol are moving away from you. They're talking and laughing as they move through the forest. They have no idea you're there.

You quietly move up behind them. Yelena draws her weapon, while you and Pyotr prepare to take the two men down from behind.

You inch closer and closer, getting ready to strike. But then, at the worst possible time, Pyotr stumbles over a tree root. The two soldiers whirl about.

It takes you half a second to realize what's happened. Your hesitation proves deadly. The trained German soldiers respond swiftly to the threat. In a heartbeat, their weapons are drawn. Your mission is a failure, and the price is your life.

THE END

To follow another path, turn to page 7.
To learn more about the Russian front, turn to page 97.

"Stay focused," you tell Yelena. "Even if we capture the scouts, what are we going to do with them? We have a plan. Let's stick to it."

Yelena glares at you. But you ignore her icy stare. You know it's the right decision.

After a few minutes, the sound of the voices fades away. You're alone.

The bridge stands before you. It crosses a small creek that runs through a deep ravine. It's the only easy way over the ravine for miles.

"What do you think?" Pyotr asks, pulling an explosive charge out of his pack.

He points to a column near the end of the bridge. The column helps support the rest of the structure. It would be easy to attach a charge there.

"I say we detonate a charge in the middle of the bridge, at its weakest point," Yelena argues.

"It's more dangerous," Pyotr responds, "And we could be spotted."

"But it's sure to destroy the structure," Yelena presses.

They both look at you to make the final decision.

- To set a charge on the column, turn to page 91.
- To set a charge in the middle, turn to page 94.

You have to act fast. Without even really thinking about it, you spring up from your position along the ridge. You draw your weapon and charge straight at the train. You raise your gun as you charge. It gets the attention of the two military trucks. They break off, both heading toward you. And they're coming fast.

You turn and run back toward the cover of the trees. But it's too late. The rattle of machine gun fire echoes across the landscape.

Yelena needed a diversion. You provided one. You gave her the chance she needed to derail the train. But it cost you your life.

THE END

To follow another path, turn to page 7.
To learn more about the Russian front, turn to page 97.

"Over here Nazi scum!" you shout.

You stand and wave your arms in the direction of the trucks. But you're too far away, and the train is too loud. They never hear you.

"Oh no," Pyotr gasps.

You both stand there in shock, realizing what you've done. The train rounds a curve, headed right into the ambush site. Then there's a sound that makes your blood run cold—machine gun fire.

You failed Yelena and her team. With no distraction, you're sure the Nazi military guard had no trouble spotting and eliminating your fellow partisans. Yelena and the others probably tried to run or hide from the German soldiers. You hope they weren't too late.

Turn the page.

The mission is a disaster. You later learn your friends are dead. Maybe you just weren't cut out to fight the Nazis. Maybe you should have left the fighting to the real soldiers.

THE END

To follow another path, turn to page 7.
To learn more about the Russian front, turn to page 97.

Everything depends on setting the charge. So you dash out behind Pyotr and Ivan. The three of you sprint across the open space alongside the tracks. As quickly as you can, you get to work, attaching the explosive to the train tracks, then setting the detonator so you can activate it from a safe distance.

Turn the page.

For a moment, you think you might make it. But as the roar of the train grows closer, you also hear the sound of a diesel engine. It's a German military truck, armed with machine guns. You're squatting in plain sight as you set up the explosive.

"Look out!" Ivan shouts. You try to dash back to the cover of the trees. But the German gunners are ready. They've spotted you, and they're already taking aim.

You had big plans. Sadly, none of them went the way you'd imagined. And you won't live to fight another day.

THE END

To follow another path, turn to page 7.
To learn more about the Russian front, turn to page 97.

Pyotr failed to detonate his grenade. That means the mission is in danger. Charging in is foolish. So instead, you raise your weapon, ready to shoot. You don't want to have to shoot anyone. That's not who you are. But that doesn't mean you can't do some damage.

Two military trucks come around the curve, just in front of the train. You fire at the tires.

And you're in luck. Your first shot hits the mark. One of the front tires on the lead truck blows, sending it skidding toward a steep embankment. Quickly, you fire at the second truck. This time, you miss the tire. But that's okay. Your shot goes straight through the truck's big diesel engine. German soldiers fling themselves off the truck as it bursts into flames.

Turn the page.

A moment later, Yelena and Ivan do their part. Their explosive charge goes off just as the train arrives. A terrible, high-pitched sound of screeching metal fills the air as the train skids off the tracks and barrels into the forest. Fuel cars burst into flames. Boxcars spill huge loads of food, weapons, and other supplies.

You take a moment to soak in the chaos before quickly disappearing into the forest.

"Score another victory for the partisans," Yelena says with a grin. You can only grin back. You're no soldier. But you're proof that anyone can help in the fight to drive the Nazi invaders out of your lands.

THE END

To follow another path, turn to page 7.
To learn more about the Russian front, turn to page 97.

You have no desire to climb out to the middle of the bridge. You'll be exposed if any other patrols come around. And there's a very real risk of falling if you can't get off the bridge quickly enough. You peer into the ravine. It's a long way down.

"I say we hit the column," you reply, taking the charge from Pyotr.

You scramble down the slope until you can reach the point where the column connects to the rest of the structure. Carefully, you attach the charge. It's the last one you have, so you have to make this count.

Once the charge is attached, the three of you run to the cover of the forest. Then comes the moment of truth. You press a button on a remote detonator to set off the charge.

Turn the page.

The explosion is impressive. It echoes across the landscape, and the bright orange glow from flames briefly lights up the forest.

Pyotr howls in celebration. But it's short-lived.

"Oh no," Yelena groans.

Your heart sinks. The bridge is still standing. The column is damaged, but not destroyed.

"All that planning, all that risk . . . for nothing," you say, stunned.

Yelena pulls on your arm. "Come on, we have to go. The Germans are surely on their way."

You run into the forest, heading back to your base. Today was a failure. Maybe you'll do better next time.

THE END

To follow another path, turn to page 7.

To learn more about the Russian front, turn to page 97.

"This time, I'm with Yelena," you say. "We only get one shot at this. We have to make sure we take down the bridge."

Pyotr shoves the charge into your arms. "Okay," he says. "Then you set the charge."

You grin nervously as you start to make your way along the outer edge of the bridge. It's a long way down, but you keep your gaze focused on your feet.

Carefully, you attach the charge to the underside of the bridge. You set the detonator and scurry back.

Suddenly, you slip. You almost lose your grip. For a moment, you're dangling over the deep ravine by one hand. With a rush of adrenaline, you pull yourself up and run back to Yelena and Pyotr.

The three of you dash off into the forest, where you press a button on the detonator to set off the charge. The blast shakes the ground and briefly lights up the sky.

"We did it!" Yelena shouts. She's right. The bridge is collapsing. Big fragments are tumbling down into the ravine.

Turn the page.

It's a small victory. The Germans can still move supplies by train, and they can use other bridges. But you've cut off one key route for their supply lines today. In war, even a small victory is something to celebrate.

THE END

To follow another path, turn to page 7.
To learn more about the Russian front, turn to page 97.

CHAPTER 5

A BLOODY FRONT

World War II was a war unlike any war before or since. While World War I was fought about 20 years earlier, technology had changed a lot in that time. The tanks, planes, and warships of the time brought in a new era of warfare. Some estimates say that 15 million soldiers and 45 million civilians died in the six-year conflict. The war stretched from Europe to Africa to the Pacific Ocean.

Some of the heaviest fighting occurred in Eastern Europe between German and Soviet forces. This was often called the Eastern front or the Russian front. Russia was the biggest republic in the Soviet Union.

Although Germany and the Soviet Union started the war with an agreement not to fight each other, Germany quickly broke it. Germany and the Axis powers tried to move swiftly, marching east into present-day Ukraine, Belarus, and other Soviet territories. The biggest part of the invasion began in 1941. It was called Operation Barbarossa. It set more than 4 million Axis troops against the Soviet Red Army, which was 5.5 million strong.

Four years of combat followed. Bombers filled the skies. Warships fought for control of the Black Sea. Tanks rumbled over frozen ground.

Early on, the Axis forces pressed deep into Soviet territory. Some of the war's most brutal battles were fought there. Among them was the Battle of Stalingrad, which claimed about 1.8 million lives. Other major battles included the Siege of Leningrad and the Battle of Berlin.

German tanks and troops advance during Operation Barbarossa in the summer of 1941.

The German forces had hoped to quickly sweep through the Soviet Union. But the Red Army fiercely defended its land. Meanwhile, civilian fighters, called partisans, hounded the Germans from behind enemy lines, attacking troops and disrupting supply lines. Partisan fighters were not part of any official military. But their efforts slowed down the invaders.

The fierce Soviet resistance forced Germany to pour more and more resources into the Eastern front. As the United States, Great Britain, and other Allies pressed from the West, the Axis Powers were spread too thin. Germany may have been able to win in the West or the East. But it couldn't win on both fronts at the same time. By 1945, the Allies had closed in on Germany from both sides. Germany had lost. They had no choice but to surrender. Adolf Hitler took his own life in defeat.

Adolf Hitler

The war in Europe was over. However, Japan continued the fight in the Pacific. As the death toll mounted, the United States took a drastic step. It unleashed a fearsome new weapon. U.S. bombers dropped the first atomic bomb on the Japanese city of Hiroshima on August 6. They dropped a second bomb on Nagasaki three days later. Both cities were destroyed. Hundreds of thousands of people died.

World War II was finally over. But the effects of the terrible war continue to this day. Leaders in Eastern countries—mainly the Soviet Union—believed that Western countries such as the United States were trying to gain influence over all of Europe. Meanwhile, many people in the West were distrustful of communism, a style of government in the Soviet Union that they felt was too controlling of its population.

As a result, Germany was split in half. West Germany came under control of the Western world and became an independent nation in 1949. Meanwhile, the Soviet Union took charge of East Germany.

Over the years that followed, the United States and the Soviet Union—once allies—became enemies. Each built up its own stores of atomic weapons.

The countries threatened to use these powerful weapons against the other side if they made political decisions the other side disagreed with. It was a time called the Cold War.

Almost 80 years later, the Soviet Union is gone. Its republics became independent countries, with Russia being the largest.

Russian distrust of the West remains today. It served as a major reason Russia invaded Ukraine in 2022. Russian leaders feared that more and more countries it once controlled were adopting Western ways and allying themselves with the United States. Some have called the war in Ukraine the worst in Europe since the end of World War II.

Tension between the West and Russia has grown. World War II is long over. But the effects of the terrible conflict echo into the modern day.

Ukrainian troops prepare to battle Russian troops on the front lines.

MAP OF THE RUSSIAN FRONT (1939)

Siege of Leningrad

Moscow

Battle of Berlin

Battle of Stalingrad

Carpathian Mountains

Black Sea

RUSSIA
(UNION OF SOVIET SOCIALIST REPUBLICS)

NORWAY

SWEDEN

FINLAND

III REICH

POLAND

CZECHOSLOVAKIA

HUNGARY

ROMANIA

YUGOSLAVIA

ITALY

BULGARIA

GREECE

TURKEY

ESTONIA

LATVIA

LITHUANIA

DENMARK

LEGEND

● BATTLES

◆ POINTS OF INTEREST

TIMELINE

Sept. 1, 1939	Germany invades Poland. World War II begins.
June 1941 to Jan. 1942	Operation Barbarossa: The Axis powers attempt to invade the Soviet Union.
Oct. 1941	Axis bombers attack the Soviet Black Sea Fleet.
Dec. 7, 1941	The Japanese bomb Pearl Harbor, Hawaii. The United States enters the war the next day.
Jan. 1942	The Soviet Army wins the Battle of Moscow.
July 1942 to Feb. 1943	The Battle of Stalingrad: 2 million casualties, the Red Army holds back the Germans.
July 5 to Aug. 23, 1943	The Battle of Kursk: It is the largest tank battle in the war. The Soviets win.
Jan. 1945	The Allies drive back the Germans, putting down the Nazi's last major offensive of the war.
May 7, 1945	Germany surrenders, ending the war in Europe
Aug. 1945	U.S. drops atomic bombs on the Japanese cities of Hiroshima and Nagasaki. Japan surrenders.

OTHER PATHS TO EXPLORE

In this book, you've explored several key operations that took place on the Eastern front during World War II. But the experiences of those who fought in these situations were just a part of what it was like to live and serve during World War II. How might your perspective change in a different situation?

1. Many ordinary civilians were caught in the middle of the fighting on the Eastern front. What would you do if enemy forces were marching through your lands? Would you fight against them? Or would you keep quiet and stay far from trouble?

2. The Axis powers took many prisoners after their battles with the Red Army. What would life be like in a German prison camp? Would you have what it takes to survive in harsh conditions? How would you survive?

3. Spies played a big role in World War II. Some Soviet spies lived deep behind enemy lines, pretending to be loyal to Germany and the other Axis powers. What would it be like to live among the enemy, gathering its secrets? Would you have what it takes to stay undetected? How might you get critical information to Soviet leaders?

GLOSSARY

ambush (AM-bush)—a surprise attack

atomic (uh-TOM-ic)—using the power created when atoms are split

casualty (KAZH-oo-uhl-tee)—a person killed, wounded, or missing in a battle or in a war

cruiser (KROO-zuhr)—a large Navy ship armed with cruise missiles, big guns, and other powerful weapons

intelligence (in-TEL-uh-jenss)—secretly gathered military information about an enemy

Nazi (NOT-see)—a member of the political party of Germany, led by Adolf Hitler, that ruled Germany from 1933 to 1945

partisan (PAR-tih-suhn)—a person who fights against an enemy force but is not formally part of a military

payload (PAY-lohd)—the total weight of items carried by an airplane; in war, missiles and bombs

surrender (suh-REN-dur)—to give up or admit defeat

torpedo boat (tor-PEE-doh BOTE)—a small, fast ship that carries explosive torpedoes into battle

SELECT BIBLIOGRAPHY

Badsey, Stephen (ed.). *The Hutchinson Atlas of World War II Battle Plans: Before and After*. Chicago: Helicon Publishing, 2000.

Dimbleby, Jonathan. *Operation Barbarossa: The History of a Cataclysm*. New York: Oxford University Press, 2021.

Roberts, Geoffrey. *Victory at Stalingrad*. New York: Routledge, 2013.

Schneider, Carl J. and Dorothy Schneider. *World War II*. New York: Facts on File, 2003.

Suermondt, Jan. *Infantry Weapons of World War II*. Minneapolis: Chartwell Books, 2012.

Stone, Norman. *World War Two: A Short History*. New York: Basic Books, 2013.

READ MORE

Dickmann, Nancy. *Fighting to Survive World War II: Terrifying True Stories.* North Mankato, MN: Compass Point Books, 2020.

Doeden, Matt. *World War II on the European Frontlines: An Interactive History Adventure.* North Mankato, MN: Capstone Press, 2023.

MacCarald, Clara. *Weapons of World War II.* Lake Elmo, MN: Focus Readers, 2023.

INTERNET SITES

Ducksters: World War II
ducksters.com/history/world_war_ii/

History for Kids: World War II
historyforkids.net/world-war-two.html

The National World War II Museum
nationalww2museum.org/learn/education/for-students/

ABOUT THE AUTHOR

Matt Doeden is a freelance author and editor from Minnesota. He's written numerous children's books on sports, music, current events, the military, extreme survival, and much more. His books *Basketball Shoes, Shorts, and Style, Dragons,* and *Could You Be a Monster Wave Surfer?* (all by Capstone Press) are Junior Library Guild selections. Doeden began his career as a sportswriter before turning to publishing. He lives in Minnesota with his wife and two children.